Scaredy Cat

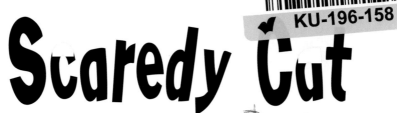

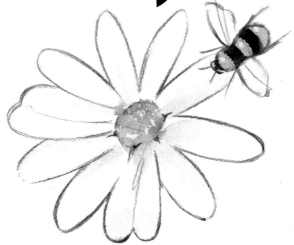

Fay Robinson

Illustrated by Mike Strudwick

RIGBY

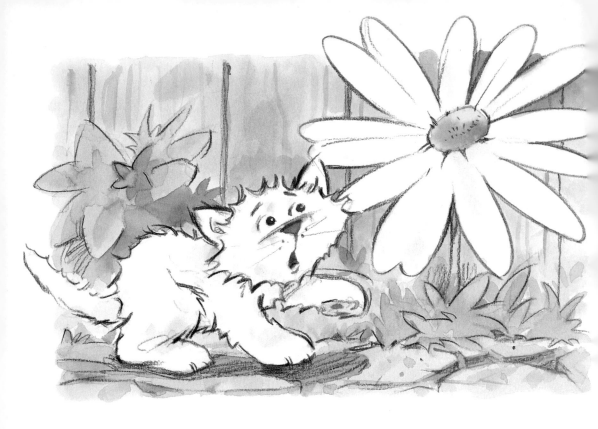

Scaredy Cat sees a flower.

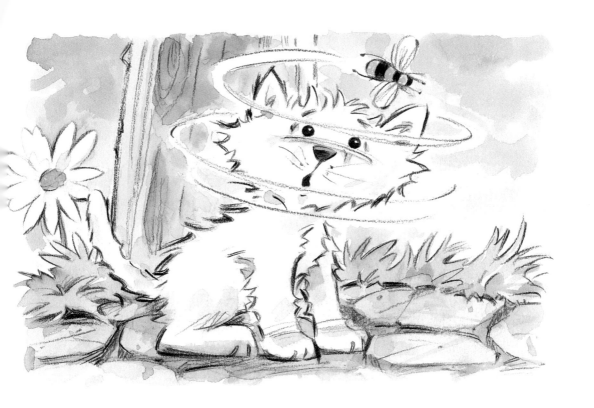

Scaredy Cat sees a bee.

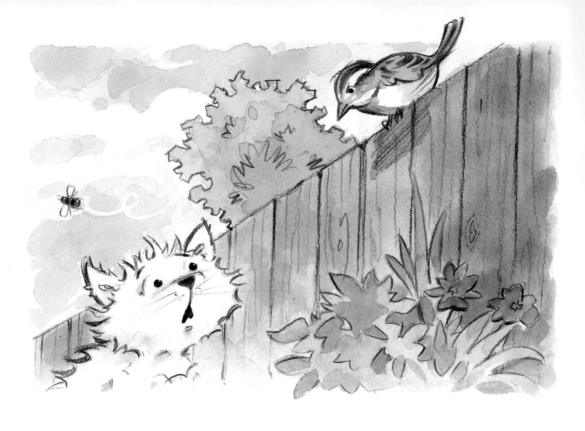

Scaredy Cat sees a bird.

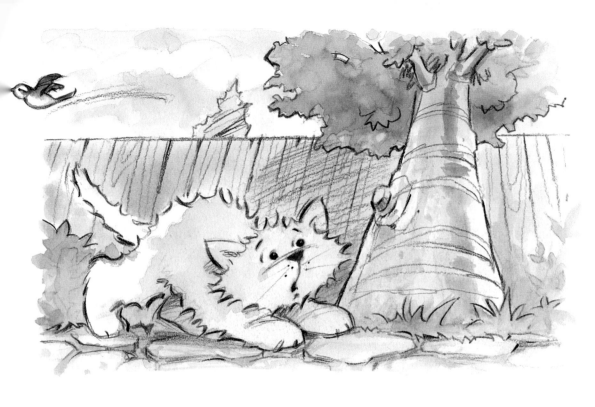

Scaredy Cat sees a tree.

5

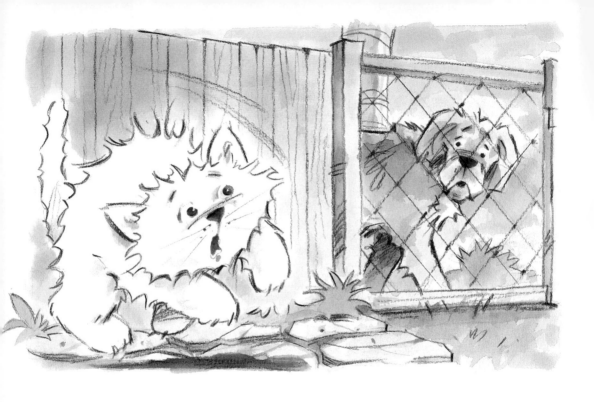

Scaredy Cat sees a dog.

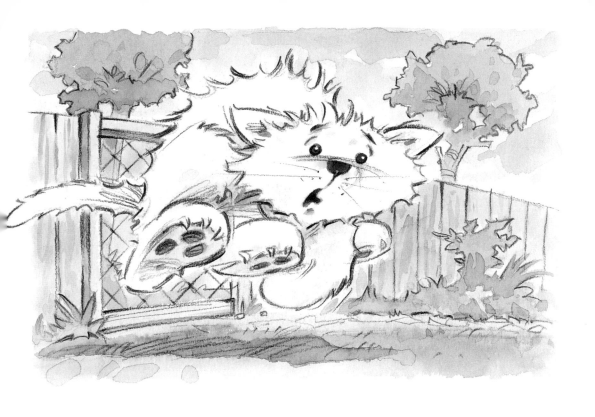

Scaredy Cat sees . . .

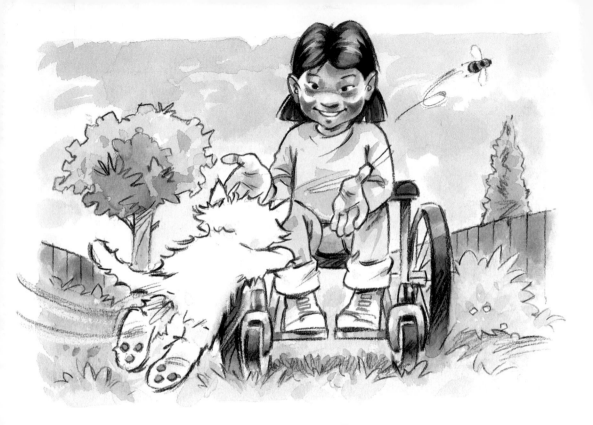

me!